DESTINED FOR GREATNESS

DR. GEORGE AGBONSON

Christ Restoration
Publications

Destined For Greatness
Dr. George Agbonson
Copyright © 2012 by Christ Restoration Publications

Christ Restoration Publications
4756 N. 70th Ave. Phoenix, AZ 85033
www.christrestoration.net

Printed in the United States of America

*Scripture text in bold is the emphasis of the author.

Sis Samantha God has
Great Plans for You. This book
will help You fulfill Your
Destiny.

Pastle George Adamson. 6/15/14

Table of Contents

INTRODUCTION

Too many people are living their lives below the margin of success. Today's generation have witnessed tremendous growth in terms of frustration and depression.

Life has become meaningless to many. Not because there is nothing more to be achieved, but they do not know what to do with their lives. College students are confused, not sure of what to do after graduation. Singles wants to get married at all cost, some are not sure if marriage is for the. The rate of divorce is alarming, it is scaring. This is because many got into marriage for the wrong reason, now they want out. To them marriage is not fun like they thought it will be. The hustler wants to get rich or at least die trying. To them that is heroic. Pastors are quitting ministry since the Ministry is not paying off as they thought it will be when they were in Bible College. Business people are frustrated, some are having cardiac arrest because all their investment has gone down the drain with the fallen economy.

Everywhere you turn, it's just issues, problems, challenges of life. Is there a better way to live? Everyone is seeking for the smartest way to be successful. It is to this end that this book comes as a timely piece for this generation and generations to come. I intend to share with every reader the blue print to success, God's way. Not just what success is, but how to get there. There is a common saying that knowledge is power but revelation- knowledge is super power.

My prayer for you is that God will fill you with unusual understanding as you read through, study, and meditate on the principles shared. And also apply them appropriately in the direction God leads you.

There are keys to everything under heaven. Jesus talked about keys in the New Testament as access to power:

> When Jesus came into the region of Caesarea Philippi, He asked His disciples, saying, "Who do men say that I, the Son of Man, am?" So they said, "Some say John the Baptist, some Elijah, and others Jeremiah or one of the prophets." He said to them, "But who do you say that I am?" Simon Peter answered and said, "You are the Christ, the Son of the living God." Jesus answered and said to him, Blessed are you, Simon Bar-Jonah, for flesh and blood has not revealed this to you, but My Father who is in heaven. And I also say to you that you are

Peter, and on this rock I will build My church, and the gates of Hades shall not prevail against it. And I will give you the keys of the kingdom of heaven, and whatever you bind on earth will be bound in heaven, and whatever you loose on earth will be loosed in heaven." Then He commanded His disciples that they should tell no one that He was Jesus the Christ.

Matt. 16:13-20 NKJV

In the above quotation, of everyone present in this discussion, only Peter received the revelation- knowledge of Jesus' true identity. Because, Peter got this revelation, he was given the keys of the Kingdom, which symbolizes possession of authority. Jesus went further to say that his assignment will not be thwarted by the kingdom of darkness. Which means revelation- knowledge will authorize you to succeed. Not only does it guarantee success, it puts you on the pedestal of victory any day, anytime. It is surest, safest, and most secured thing to have. This book is based on revelation- knowledge, the key we all need to succeed. The keys you will learn in this book are predicated on the principles of the kingdom to be manifested on earth. So get ready for you are on your way to success in whichever area in your life you need God to help you succeed.

PART ONE

VISION

CHAPTER ONE

UNDERSTANDING VISION

There is a need to understanding what vision is. Most times when people talk about vision, they tend to be myopic about it. Vision is a mental picture of what the future holds. Vision is, today pregnant with tomorrow. Vision is destiny incubated in the now. Anyone who has a vision has a future, and those who don't have it have nothing to live for or die for. Vision is the catalyst for success. Dr. Myles Munroe puts it this way: "A vision is an idea inspired by God. It is what God wants you to contribute to the world. A vision is a picture of where you want to end up. It is like a blueprint of a finished product that you are about to produce."

Vision is likened to a remote control that decides what people watch. It determines the destiny of an individual, career, organization, family, society, nation, etc. It directs the affairs of people. Vision is the vehicle that transports you into your God-given destiny. It brings the decree of heaven to manifest on earth. Take a look at this scripture:

After these things the word of the LORD came to Abram in a vision, saying, "Do not be afraid, Abram. I am your shield, your exceedingly great reward." But Abram said, "Lord GOD, what will You give me, seeing I go childless, and the heir of my house is Eliezer of Damascus?" Then Abram said, "Look, You have given me no offspring; indeed one born in my house is my heir!" And behold, the word of the LORD came to him, saying, "This one shall not be your heir, but one who will come from your own body shall be your heir." Then He brought him outside and said, "Look now toward heaven, and count the stars if you are able to number them." And He said to him, "So shall your descendants be."And he believed in the LORD, and He accounted it to him for righteousness. Then He said to him, "I am the LORD, who brought you out of Ur of the Chaldeans, to give you this land to inherit it." Gen. 15:1-7 NKJV

The Lord told Abram to gaze into his future from his present state. In essence God wanted Abram to see where he was going in order for him to have faith. And then, please God. This means Christians with God-given vision are believers having faith, they please God. And they accomplish great things on earth. Every achiever is a visionary. You will never be celebrated until you are a vision carrier. A visionary is automatically a leader. Many times people fight to get to the top, but what helps you climb the ladder of success is vision. Vision is the beginning of every great journey. You can tell where a person will end by the vision they're running with.

It is a waste of time, energy, resources to work with people that are visionless. I once talked to a Pastor who said he served in a ministry for over fifteen years. And he felt he wasted that fifteen years of his life because he felt he was in obscurity. He didn't know where he was going or the destination of the ministry. Eventually, he resigned from that ministry, and his whole life changed for good.

I strongly believe that people without vision will end up in frustration, unfulfilled, and unhappy. A lot of marriages run into crisis because they lack the vision for the marriage. Can I suggest to you not to do anything, or make any major decision in your life, without first knowing what the blueprint is. Divine vision is the blueprint you need to achieve success in life.

I one time had a smart phone that was so touchy. Now, this cell phone was very sophisticated, but I had a lot of problems with it because I couldn't figure out how to use it effectively. One day I got so frustrated with it, and almost smashed it on the floor. And a friend of mine who saw my frustration asked me, did you ever read the manual? Truthfully speaking I never read the manual. There is a popular saying that men don't like read manuals or follow instruction books. I don't know how true that is, but I can tell you this much that I suffered using my phone as a result of ignorance. Not because the information wasn't provided but I ignored it. Do you know that a lot of people are living their lives without understanding the blueprint of their destinies?

Everyone created by God was created to fulfill a purpose on earth. No one was born a failure or born to fail. It is disheartening to God to see that people die without fulfilling their destinies. You are specially, uniquely, and fearfully made. Vision is the package. All you need to do is to unwrap it. That is the very reason why you are reading this book right now. You are pregnant with a vision, what you do to that pregnancy will determine if you will eventually deliver, or miscarry.

Now I must establish here that not all vision are God-given vision. Every vision has a source, and the source of the vision determines the end result. Of course a positive vision will benefit humanity, while a negative vision destroys humanity. But the purpose of this book is to stir up the God-given vision inside of you, teaching you how to give birth to your dream.

1. Devine Vision

CHAPTER TWO

THE VISIONARY GOD

It takes a visionary to create another visionary. God is a visionary God. One of his names is "Alpha & Omega" – The first and the last, the beginning and the ending (Rev.1:8). This literally means He remains God from the very beginning to the end. He is outside time, not confined to time, lives in eternity. Nothing can change him, add to Him, or reduce Him. He is who He is. That is the very reason why he can speaks the end from the beginning. He finishes before he even starts. This is so powerful, it means whatever that emanates from God stands sure. It must deliver, not even the problems in-between can hinder it, because, our God is a visionary God. This is seen all through Scripture. And if we understand this concept, it will be easy to understand why we have to be visionary as well. **Vision is the ability to see what others don't see**. God happens to be that way as seen in the creation story:

In the beginning God created the heavens and the earth. The earth was without form, and void; and darkness was on the face of the deep. And the Spirit of God was hovering over the face of the waters. Then God said,

16

"Let there be light"; and there was light. And God saw the light, that it was good; and God divided the light from the darkness. God called the light Day, and the darkness He called Night. So the evening and the morning were the first day. Then God said, "Let there be a firmament in the midst of the waters, and let it divide the waters from the waters." Thus God made the firmament, and divided the waters which were under the firmament from the waters which were above the firmament; and it was so. And God called the firmament Heaven. So the evening and the morning were the second day. Then God said, "Let the waters under the heavens be gathered together into one place, and let the dry land appear"; and it was so. And God called the dry land Earth, and the gathering together of the waters He called Seas. And God saw that it was good. Then God said, "Let the earth bring forth grass, the herb that yields seed, and the fruit tree that yields fruit according to its kind, whose seed is in itself, on the earth"; and it was so. And the earth brought forth grass, the herb that yields seed according to its kind, and the tree that yields fruit, whose seed is in itself according to its kind. And God saw that it was good. So the evening and the morning were the third day. Then God said,

"Let there be lights in the firmament of the heavens to divide the day from the night; and let them be for signs and seasons, and for days and years; and let them be for lights in the firmament of the heavens to give light on the earth"; and it was so. Then God made two great lights: the greater light to rule the day, and the lesser light to rule the night. He made the stars also. God set them in the firmament of the heavens to give light on the earth, and to rule over the day and over the night, and to divide the light from the darkness. And God saw that it was good. So the evening and the morning were the fourth day. Then God said, "Let the waters abound with an abundance of living creatures, and let birds fly above the earth across the face of the firmament of the heavens." So God created great sea creatures and every living thing that moves, with which the waters abounded, according to their kind, and every winged bird according to its kind. And God saw that it was good. And God blessed them, saying, "Be fruitful and multiply, and fill the waters in the seas, and let birds multiply on the earth." So the evening and the morning were the fifth day. Then God said, "Let the earth bring forth the living creature according to its kind: cattle and creeping thing and beast of the earth, each according to its kind"; and it was so. And God made the beast of the earth according to its kind, cattle according to its kind, and everything that creeps on the earth according to its kind. And God saw that it was good.

Then God said, "Let Us make man in Our image, according to Our likeness; let them have dominion over the fish of the sea, over the birds of the air, and over the cattle, over all the earth and over every creeping thing that creeps on the earth." So God created man in His own image; in the image of God He created him; male and female He created them. Then God blessed them, and God said to them, "Be fruitful and multiply; fill the earth and subdue it; have dominion over the fish of the sea, over the birds of the air, and over every living thing that moves on the earth. Genesis 1:1-228 NKJV

It takes only a visionary to do what God did in Genesis. The earth was in chaos, desolation, empty, void. All you could see at that time was water everywhere. But the Holy Spirit moved on the water. In fact the Hebrew word used is, 'rachaph' which means to brood; by implication, to be relaxed. What happened here could be likened to a chicken who is about to hatch her eggs. She relaxes on her eggs, broods on it, wait for her chick to come forth. No matter what comes her way, she must try to remain focus and purposeful. This is the incubation stage before hatching.

The Holy Spirit incubated on the water with a vision in the mind of God. Although the world was filled with water but the visionary God saw land buried beneath the water, beneath the water were trees, the trees was pregnant with fruits and leaves, the water was pregnant with fishes and other sea creatures, the land was destined to inhabit mankind, animals, other creatures, the sky also needed companion of birds.

What have you been destined to accomplish that is yet to manifest in your life? I believe God have you reading this book because your time has come. One of the greatest things that can happen to you is for you to see your future in the making.

Do you know that God saw the redemption of humanity before the temptation and fall in Genesis 3. This also speaks of him as being a visionary. I believe this is one of the most important manifestation of God in the restoration of humanity back to himself.

So the LORD God said to the serpent: because you have done this, you are cursed more than all cattle, and more than every beast of the field; on your belly you shall go, and you shall eat dust all the days of your life. and I will put enmity between you and the woman, and between your seed and her Seed; **He shall bruise your head, and you shall bruise His heel.**
Genesis 3:14-15 NKJV

The highlighted phrase in the above sentence is the first prophecy spoken about Christ in the Bible. This was the vision of God downloaded to humanity. Although, Satan thought he got God's creature, mankind. But God had something planned out. Jesus Christ will eventually come to redeem man. This will be through bruising which was the crucifixion and death of Christ, and the seed bruising of the head symbolizes the victory of Christ over Satan through his resurrection.

Now you can connect the dot with what was said in the book of Revelation: *"All who dwell on the earth will worship him, whose names have not been written in the Book of Life of the Lamb slain from the foundation of the world."* Revelation 13:8 NKV

The book of Genesis spoke the vision of God concerning redemption of humanity, while the book of revelation traced it back to God's intent before Genesis was written, up till the final manifestation of the vision. This means, Christ had already been slained before man sinned. Why? God already knew the end from the beginning about the fall of man, and provided atonement before man sinned. This means nothing took God by surprise. The coming of Christ was a fulfillment of that which has been completed in heaven. This I explained in details in my other book "Journey of Faith".

The bottom line is that God had a vision of bringing mankind back to himself, he spoke the vision as a prophecy into existence, and he wrought it into manifestation. In fact, we are still working our way towards the consummation of total restoration. You see, the course of this world is only working according to divine order connected to the overall vision of restoration.

After Genesis 3, every other event was a shadow, and pointed to the coming of Christ until the appointed time.

Now I say that the heir, as long as he is a child, does not differ at all from a slave, though he is master of all, but is under guardians and stewards until the time appointed by the father. Even so we, when we were children, were in bondage under the elements of the world. But when the fullness of the time had come, God sent forth His Son, born of a woman, born under the law, to redeem those who were under the law, that we might receive the adoption as sons. And because you are sons, God has sent forth the Spirit of His Son into your hearts, crying out, "Abba, Father!" Therefore you are no longer a slave but a son, and if a son, then an heir of God through Christ.

Galatians 4:1-7

Vision steered the course of history. This was the major reason why between the prophecy and fulfillment, God protected everyone who were key players in the plans of God. They were those who were divinely chosen to be part of the history of restoration: Noah, Abraham, Joseph, Moses, David until the manifestation of the Christ, and the Church after the manifestation of the Christ until the consummation of all things.

We would examine these bible characters who were visionaries in our subsequent chapters. You just keep reading.

God wants us to be visionary like him. A goat will give birth to a goat, a dog will give birth to a dog. We reproduce after our kind right? Alright, God made us in his own image and likeness, which means we ought to look like our creator. So, why do a lot of people lack vision? Or go unfulfilled? Because, Satan tampered with this special treasure in man.

Now, I need you hear what God is saying to you today. You were not born to be miserable in life. You were not called to fail. You were not created to be defeated. You were born to fulfill destiny. Here what the word of God says, *"For I know the thoughts that I think toward you, saith the LORD, thoughts of peace, and not of evil, to give you an expected."* Jeremiah 29:11 KJV

CHAPTER THREE

MEN OF VISION IN THE BIBLE

We've learnt that our God is a visionary God, and He raises visionaries as well. You cannot accomplish anything for God until you are a visionary as well. A visionary sees what God sees. All through the Bible the great accomplishers were all visionaries. In this chapter we will highlight few characters who played a major role in the overall redemptive plan of God for humanity:

NOAH: Noah was a vision carrier, born in a generation of perverseness and darkness, yet God kept him and his family clean in order to protect the seed of righteousness. *"This is the account of Noah and his family. Noah was a righteous man, the only blameless person living on earth at the time, and he walked in close fellowship with God."* Genesis 6:9 NKJV

In the midst of perversion, Noah was chosen, set apart for divine assignment. In the midst of judgment with the flood in Genesis 7, his family and the animals survived all because of vision. Noah saw something others couldn't see.

He was instructed to build an ark in a time when people had not seen rain. Take a look at this:

Build a large boat from cypress wood and waterproof it with tar, inside and out. Then construct decks and stalls throughout its interior. Make the boat 450 feet long, 75 feet wide, and 45 feet high. Leave an 18-inch opening below the roof all the way around the boat. Put the door on the side, and build three decks inside the boat—lower, middle, and upper. "Look! I am about to cover the earth with a flood that will destroy every living thing that breathes. Everything on earth will die. But I will confirm my covenant with you. So enter the boat—you and your wife and your sons and their wives. Bring a pair of every kind of animal—a male and a female—into the boat with you to keep them alive during the flood. Pairs of every kind of bird, and every kind of animal, and every kind of small animal that scurries along the ground, will come to you to be kept alive. And be sure to take on board enough food for your family and for all the animals." So Noah did everything exactly as God had commanded him. Genesis 6:14-22

Noah's generation had not seen rain when he was asked to build an ark. My God! What kind of faith is that? That was probably the reason why nobody beside his family supported him. They mocked him, he looked insane to many. But, one thing we must learn from this man of faith is that he had a vision, a God-given vision, he kept focus. As a result, he fulfilled destiny. His family was saved amongst many. Noah's role was to preserve the seed of righteousness in his generation. There are many today who wouldn't do what God has called them to do, because of what people, family, friends would say. You might be jeopardizing the future of your family by disobeying God.

Just like Noah, you might be the deliverer sent to this generation, light in the midst of darkness. It's time to let your light shine.

ABRAHAM: The baton was handed down to Abram when he was called out of his hometown, family to an unknown place where God had destined.

Now the LORD had said to Abram: "Get out of your country, From your family and from your father's house, to a land that I will show you. I will make you a great nation; I will bless you and make your name great; and you shall be a blessing. I will bless those who bless you, and I will curse him who curses you; and in you all the families of the earth shall be blessed." So Abram departed as the LORD had spoken to him, and Lot went with him. And Abram was seventy-five years old when he departed from Haran. Then Abram took Sarai his wife and Lot his brother's son, and all their possessions that they had gathered, and the people whom they had acquired in Haran, and they departed to go to the land of Canaan. So they came to the land of Canaan. Genesis 12:1-5 NKJV

Unknown to Abram, he was a vision carrier. Probably that was why God allowed him to go through his childless state for a long time (Gen.15). You see, for every vision there is a time of preparation. The greater the vision, the tougher the preparation.

We saw the fleshly Abram stumbling by impregnating his slave Hagar, lied about his wife in Egypt, yet he was chosen and God was not going to change his mind. Listen to what God declared:

When Abram was ninety-nine years old, the LORD appeared to Abram and said to him, "I am Almighty

God; walk before Me and be blameless. And I will make My covenant between Me and you, and will multiply you exceedingly." Then Abram fell on his face, and God talked with him, saying: **As for Me**, behold, My covenant is with you, and you shall be a father of many nations." Genesis 17:1-4 NKJV

God re-enacted his covenant with this same man who had failed, and was unfaithful. The phrase in bold "As for Me" speaks of God's faithfulness that cannot fail. Now, that is the power of vision. God in his power has what it takes to sustain his own vision. He wasn't going to let any man jeopardize what he had already finished in heaven before releasing it to earth.

There are some who think they are not worthy, unqualified to be God's visionary. Yes, we are not worthy truly, but it's not about us but about Him who gave the vision.

Eventually, the unqualified Abraham delivered the seed of promise, Isaac (Gen.21). You will deliver your vision in the name of Jesus. Every divine seed inside of you must come to manifestation. Your dream must be fulfilled in Jesus name.

Abraham's role in the overall vision of God is to give birth to the chosen people through whom the Messiah would be revealed.

JOSEPH: That of Joseph was very pathetic. He was loved by his father more than his other brothers. He was a vision carrier, yet he was hated by his brothers which eventually led him to slavery in a foreign land.

Now Jacob dwelt in the land where his father was a stranger, in the land of Canaan. This is the history of Jacob. Joseph, being seventeen years old, was feeding the flock with his brothers. And the lad was with the sons of Bilhah and the sons of Zilpah, his father's wives; and Joseph brought a bad report of them to his father. Now Israel loved Joseph more than all his children, because he was the son of his old age. Also he made him a tunic of many colors. But when his brothers saw that their father loved him more than all his brothers, they hated him and could not speak peaceably to him. Now Joseph had a dream, and he told it to his brothers; and they hated him even more. So he said to them, "Please hear this dream which I have dreamed: There we were, binding sheaves in the field. Then behold, my sheaf arose and also stood upright; and indeed your sheaves stood all around and bowed down to my sheaf." And his brothers said to him, "Shall you indeed reign over us? Or shall you indeed have dominion over us?" So they hated him even more for his dreams and for his words. Genesis 37:1-8 NKJV

Probably, the young man Joseph would have been wondering why he went through so much trauma in his life? Not only was he sold as a slave by his brothers. He was lied on by Potiphar's wife which led to his imprisonment (Gen. 39). Not again! Yet, God had a hand in all of these. It was through his imprisonment, he will be promoted to the throne (Gen.40). This eventually brought his dream to fulfillment. He became the prime minister of Egypt. Then the famine led the children of Israel to Egypt. Eventually, they bowed to the one who had the key of survival at that time. His name was Joseph, the one hated by his brothers, sold to slavery, the dreamer (Gen.44-46).

When you are a visionary, you go through so much unlike others. You feel so different. Yes, that is how it is. You are different. Most of the challenges you undergo is not necessarily for you but it is the pathway to your destiny.

The lesson learnt from all of those experiences will eventually help you in your future assignment.

Looking at the broader picture, the reason why God allowed these things to happen to Joseph was to fulfill his promise he made to Abraham:

> "Now when the sun was going down, a deep sleep fell upon Abram; and behold, horror and great darkness fell upon him. Then He said to Abram: "Know certainly that your descendants will be strangers in a land that is not theirs, and will serve them, and they will afflict them four hundred years. And also the nation whom they serve I will judge; afterward they shall come out with great possessions."
>
> Genesis 15:12-14 NKJV

Joseph's part in the prophetic fulfillment was to bring the Israelites to Egypt where they will eventually be formed as a nation. All along, Joseph was only fulfilling destiny.

MOSES: After the children of Israel had grown into a formidable size, and fulfilled their days in Egypt according to the word of the Lord, it was time to bring them out. God raised another visionary called Moses. Now, everything about Moses from birth to death was mysterious. His life was orchestrated by God. All of these happened for one purpose: Moses was born to fulfill his destiny, as a deliverer:

Now it happened in the process of time that the king of Egypt died. Then the children of Israel groaned because of the bondage, and they cried out; and their cry came up to God because of the bondage. So God heard their groaning, and God remembered His covenant with Abraham, with Isaac, and with Jacob. And God looked upon the children of Israel, and God acknowledged them. Exodus 2:23-25 NKJV.

It was a difficult process for Moses as well. He didn't understand why he was demoted from being the celebrity to a fugitive, from a palace prince to wilderness shepherd. This was a sharp contrast, yet he was to discover his purpose or calling in the wilderness not in the palace:

Now Moses was tending the flock of Jethro his father-in-law, the priest of Midian. And he led the flock to the back of the desert, and came to Horeb, the mountain of God. And the Angel of the LORD appeared to him in a flame of fire from the midst of a bush. So he looked, and behold, the bush was burning with fire, but the bush was not consumed. Then Moses said, "I will now turn aside and see this great sight, why the bush does not burn."So when the LORD saw that he turned aside to look, God called to him from the midst of the bush and said, "Moses, Moses!" And he said, "Here I am." Then He said, "Do not draw near this place. Take your sandals off your feet, for the place where you stand is holy ground." Moreover He said, "I am the God of your father—the God of Abraham, the God of Isaac, and the God of Jacob." And Moses hid his face, for he was afraid to look upon God. And the LORD said: "I have surely seen the oppression of My people who are in Egypt, and have heard their cry because of their taskmasters, for I know their sorrows. So I have come down to deliver them out of the hand of the Egyptians, and to bring them up from that land to a good and large land, to a land flowing with milk and honey, to the place of the Canaanites and the Hittites and the Amorites and the Perizzites and the Hivites and the Jebusites. Now therefore, behold, the cry of the children of Israel has come to Me, and I have also seen the oppression with which the Egyptians oppress them. Come now, therefore, and I will send you to Pharaoh that you may bring My people, the children of Israel, out of Egypt."

Exodus 3:1-10 NKJV.

Moses found his purpose in the wilderness not in the palace. Does this relate to you? All your misfortune, disappointment, failures is to help you find your calling. This is a true sign of a visionary.

Moses role was to get the nation of Israel out of Egypt, lead through the wilderness which is the path to their destination, Canaan.

DAVID: This is one major character we must pay close attention to. He was not just elected by men, but chosen by God after the disobedience of King Saul. David was the only King God referred to as a man after his heart. "And when He had removed him, He raised up for them David as king, to whom also He gave testimony and said, 'I have found David[a]the son of Jesse, a man after My own heart, who will do all My will" Acts 13:22 NKJV

David wasn't a righteous man so to speak. He committed murder and adultery (2 Samuel 11). But he knew what God wanted, he understood the vision of God. The first thing he did when he became King was to restore the ark of covenant that was stolen back to Jerusalem (2 Samuel 6), after that, he decided to build the temple that was destroyed for God (2 Samuel 7). This is truly a man after God's heart. Hear what God thought was about David:

Now it came to pass when the king was dwelling in his house, and the LORD had given him rest from all his enemies all around, that the king said to Nathan the prophet, "See now, I dwell in a house of cedar, but the ark of God dwells inside tent curtains."Then Nathan said to the king, "Go, do all that is in your heart, for the LORD is with you." But it happened that night that the word of the LORD came to Nathan, saying, "Go and tell My servant David, 'Thus says the LORD: "Would you build a house for Me to dwell in? For I have not dwelt in a house since the time that I brought the children of Israel up from Egypt, even to this day, but have moved about in a tent and in a tabernacle. Wherever I have moved about with all the children of Israel, have I ever spoken a word to anyone from the tribes of Israel, whom I commanded to shepherd My people Israel, saying, 'Why have you not built Me a house of cedar?'"' Now therefore, thus shall you say to My servant David, 'Thus says the LORD of hosts: "I took you from the sheepfold, from following the sheep, to be ruler over My people, over Israel. And I have been with you wherever you have gone, and have cut off all your enemies from before you, and have made you a great name, like the name of the great men who are on the earth. Moreover I will appoint a place for My people Israel, and will plant them, that they may dwell in a place of their own and move no more; nor shall the sons of wickedness oppress them anymore, as previously, since the time that I commanded judges to be over My people Israel, and have caused you to rest from all your enemies. Also the LORD tells you that He will make you a house. "When your days are fulfilled and you rest with your fathers, I will set up your seed after you, who will come from your body, and I will establish his kingdom. He shall build a house for My name, and I will establish the throne of his kingdom forever. I will be his Father, and he shall be My son. If he commits iniquity, I will chasten him with the rod of men and with the blows of the sons of men. But My mercy shall not depart from him, as I took it from Saul, whom I removed from before you. And your house and your kingdom shall be established forever before you. Your throne shall be established forever."

David understood his role in the overall vision of God and fulfilled it. His reign as King was to typify the future reign of our Lord Jesus in establishing his Kingdom on earth. That was why the coming of Jesus as King was to be built upon the dynasty of David. Now we can connect the dot why Jesus was referred to in the New Testament as "Son of David".

Would you make up your mind today to do all of God's will. Become God's partner in His Kingdom building on earth, and watch God bless you and your generation just like David did?

CHAPTER FOUR

ESSENTIALS OF VISION

"Without prophetic vision people run wild, but blessed are those who follow God's teachings."
Proverbs 29:18 GOD'S WORD Translation.

I don't know how people can live their lives without a vision. To be visionless is to be purposeless. The above translation says people without vision run wild, no direction, no destination. So you can imagine why there is so much frustration at an alarming rate including suicide.

I must stress here that not all pictures are visions. Like John Graham says, "A vision is not a vague wish or dream or hope. It's a picture of the real results of real efforts." Many at times people hope for a better tomorrow and feel they have a vision. No, that's not the case. Every vision must have some specific ingredients to be real vision. Let's examine some ingredients for godly vision:

1. Vision Sets the Stage for Adventure:

Anytime God is set to do anything great on earth he stirs up the heart of somebody for an adventure that can sometime be a lifetime.

Now in the first year of Cyrus king of Persia, that the word of the LORD by the mouth of Jeremiah might be fulfilled, the LORD stirred up the spirit of Cyrus king of Persia, so that he made a proclamation throughout all his kingdom, and also put it in writing, saying All the kingdoms of the earth the LORD God of heaven has given me. And He has commanded me to build Him a house at Jerusalem which is in Judah. Who is among you of all His people? May his God be with him, and let him go up to Jerusalem which is in Judah, and build the house of the LORD God of Israel (He is God), which is in Jerusalem.

Ezra 1:1-3 NKJV.

A godly vision gets people ready for something incredible. A godly vision is always beyond you. If it is something you could do easily, then it's not a vision from God. A vision from God provides the room for God to prove himself. It is always beyond and above you. That's why it is from God. You will never grow beyond your vision. Find somebody who has a greater vision than you and plug yourself in if you will want to attain greatness.

2. Vision has the Propensity to Lead:

Since vision is the blueprint to fulfilling destiny, then it must have what it takes to lead others. A visionary has the ability, capability to carry others along towards its fulfillment. There can't be any good governance in a nation except the leader is a visionary. Show me an organization, church that is thriving today. I will show you a visionary leader. This is one reason why you must be cautious of who leads you.

Now in the second month of the second year of their coming to the house of God at Jerusalem, Zerubbabel the son of Shealtiel, Jeshua the son of Jozadak, and the rest of their brethren the priests and the Levites, and all those who had come out of the captivity to Jerusalem, began work and appointed the Levites from twenty years old and above to oversee the work of the house of the LORD. Then Jeshua with his sons and brothers, Kadmiel with his sons, and the sons of Judah, arose as one to oversee those working on the house of God: the sons of Henadad with their sons and their brethren the Levites. When the builders laid the foundation of the temple of the LORD, the priests stood in their apparel with trumpets, and the Levites, the sons of Asaph, with cymbals, to praise the LORD, according to the ordinance of David king of Israel. And they sang responsively, praising and giving thanks to the LORD: "For He is good, For His mercy endures forever toward Israel." Then all the people shouted with a great shout, when they praised the LORD, because the foundation of the house of the LORD was laid

Ezra 3:8-11 NKJV

3. Vision Brings Opposition:

Every time God gives a vision, it will arouse satanic opposition. Satan is anti-God and oppose to anything good. One way to know you are on track is the opposition you receive. The size of the vision determines the level of attacks.

Now when the adversaries of Judah and Benjamin heard that the descendants of the were building the temple of the LORD God of Israel, they came to Zerubbabel and the heads of the fathers' houses, and said to them, "Let us build with you, for we seek your God as you do; and we have sacrificed to Him since the days of Esarhaddon king of Assyria, who brought us here." But Zerubbabel and Jeshua and the rest of the heads of the fathers' houses of Israel said to them, "You may do nothing with us to build a house for our God; but we alone will build to the LORD God of Israel, as King Cyrus the king of Persia has commanded us." Then the people of the land tried to discourage the people of Judah. They troubled them in building, and hired counselors against them to frustrate their purpose all the days of Cyrus king of Persia, even until the reign of Darius king of Persia. Ezra 4:1-5 NKJV

4. Vision brings Provision:

Most times, Christians pray the wrong prayers when it comes to wealth, material prosperity, or supernatural blessings. God is not a waster. He is too purposeful to fail. God always gives provisions proportionate to his vision. When you ask God for a million dollars, he gives a vision worth a million dollars because vision has within itself the power to pull in the resources needed. Rich people without vision end up losing their riches. Vision has the capability to sustain wealth. The only thing that keeps supply coming is vision. If you are reading this book and you are believing God for provision, it's time to start asking God for the vision that can bring the supply you need. People will support you to the extent of your vision. How big is your vision? How big is your dream?

And all those who were around them encouraged them with articles of silver and gold, with goods and livestock, and with precious things, besides all that was willingly offered. King Cyrus also brought out the articles of the house of the LORD, which Nebuchadnezzar had taken from Jerusalem and put in the temple of his gods; and Cyrus king of Persia brought them out by the hand of Mithredath the treasurer, and counted them out to Sheshbazzar the prince of Judah. This is the number of them: thirty gold platters, one thousand silver platters, twenty-nine knives, thirty gold basins, four hundred and ten silver basins of a similar kind, and one thousand other articles. All the articles of gold and silver were five thousand four hundred. All these Sheshbazzar took with the captives who were brought from Babylon to Jerusalem. Ezra 1:6-11 NKJV

5. Vision brings Motivation:

Every once in a while, people get discouraged, depressed, laid back for so many reasons. Where there is a divine assignment to be accomplished, God will always speak his word of encouragement, and motivates his people not to give up until they accomplish the mission. This is likened to prophecy. One of the purpose of prophecy is to encourage and motivate. If you have a vision, it will always motivate people to keep going. When people stop attending church they need a visionary, revivalist to stir up the fire in them. A visionary church filled with visionary people can never die.

So the elders of the Jews built, and they prospered through the prophesying of Haggai the prophet and Zechariah the son of Iddo. And they built and finished it, according to the commandment of the God of Israel, and according to the command of Cyrus, Darius, and Artaxerxes king of Persia. Now the temple was finished on the third day of the month of Adar, which was in the sixth year of the reign of King Darius. Then the children of Israel, the priests and the Levites and the rest of the descendants of the captivity, celebrated the dedication of this house of God with joy. And they offered sacrifices at the dedication of this house of God, one hundred bulls, two hundred rams, four hundred lambs, and as a sin offering for all Israel twelve male goats, according to the number of the tribes of Israel. Ezra 6:14-17 NKJV.

Now I prophesy over ever discouraged person reading this book, "Receive the strength to carry on. You will finish every project you have started in Jesus name. Be restored".

PART TWO

PURPOSE

CHAPTER ONE

RIGHTLY POSITIONED

Alignment is very important. When the wheel of a vehicle is out of alignment the driver will notice the vehicle swaying out of lane, and if not controlled the vehicle will end up in the ditch. Out of alignment causes the vehicle to lose the thread on the tire, and also loses gas fast. All of these happen because the wheel of a vehicle is out of alignment.

Do you know that there are many people today whose lives are out of alignment? They are displaced out of purpose and as a result the wind of frustration blows them to whatever direction life throws at them. If you will make it in life you've got to be purpose driven. And you cannot be purpose driven until you are rightly positioned. Like my friend, Dr. Kervin Smith says, "You cannot give birth with your legs closed, you must expose yourself." I remember when my wife was pregnant with my son Joshua. When the time came for Joshua to be born, the water broke. We dashed to the hospital and she was placed in the room to dilate. Because, though she thought she was ready but they needed the cervix to open wide enough for the baby to come out, this is called 'Labor'. We have too many people who wants to give birth to their dreams, visions, miracles, yet, they don't want to go through labor. Labor gets you in position for giving birth. That is why many die with unborn dreams and aspiration. As you read through this pages, ask yourself am I in out of alignment in my purpose? Am I running from the labor of success?

Ways To Know if You are Out of Alignment:

1.   You are only surviving and not living:
When you just want the day to go by. Nothing to accomplish in your everyday life. All you say: Today is gone, tomorrow is another day. Each day come as a virgin. It's up to you get it impregnated. God wants us to live and not just survive. *"The thief does not come except to steal, and to kill, and to destroy. I have come that they may have life, and that they may have it more abundantly."* John 10:10 NKJV

2. Not maximizing your time: Time is so precious. The difference between achievers and failures is what they do with their time. Many things can be recovered, but not time. You can lose money, cars, houses, and still recover them with time. But time is something that has so much power to dictate your destiny. Don't let anyone waste your time. Every seconds, minutes, hour, day, year counts. With time, you are either closer to your fulfillment or very far from your destiny. Time wasters are destiny killers. This is why time began with creation. *"In the beginning God created the heavens and the earth."* Genesis 1:1 NKJV. The Hebrew word is: *'re'shiyth'* which denotes time as the umbrella of everything created. All creation is subject to time. The only person outside time is God. He is infinite. You and I are finite beings and what we do with our time matters a lot.

3. Not maximizing your potential: Everyone created by God was created with some kind of potential, skill, talents, gifts. Your potential is the tool God has equipped you with to fulfill your destiny. When you receive Jesus into your life, and you abide in him. One of the regenerated work done in you by the Holy Spirit is to rejuvenate every gifts, potential you have in you.

You are gifted if you can easily do what others can't naturally. What do you enjoy doing that others benefit from? You have to learn how to turn your potential loosed to produce or deliver wealth to you. You were born to reign not to slave. We will go deeper in this in the next chapter.

4. Wrong Environment: Most entrepreneurs, pioneers, knows what it means to have the right product, concept, in the wrong location. The environment you find yourself will determine if you will ever manifest. Jesus himself experienced this. He couldn't accomplish much in his hometown like he did in other places.

> Now it came to pass, when Jesus had finished these parables, He departed from there. When He had come to His own country, He taught them in their synagogue, so that they were astonished and said, "Where did this Man get this wisdom and these mighty works? Is this not the carpenter's son? Is not His mother called Mary? And His brothers James, Joses, Simon, and Judas? And His sisters, are they not all with us? Where then did this Man get all these things?" So they were offended at Him. But Jesus said to them, "A prophet is not without honor except in his own country and in his own house." Now He did not do many mighty works there because of their unbelief. Matthew 13:53-58 NKJV

Anytime you feel this way, that you are living beneath your potential, it means God wants you to reposition yourself. Until you relocate and find the environment ordained for you, you will never fulfill your destiny. When you are in the right environment, everything you do will be appreciated. Find where you are appreciated and not tolerated.

5. Wrong People: The kind of people you surround yourself with will either make you or mar you. *"He who walks with wise men will be wise, But the companion of fools will be destroyed."* Proverbs 13:20 NKJV.

If the people who around you think below your, it means you will be limited. You are surrounded with mediocrity. And until you break away from mediocrity you will never fulfill your destiny. You need people who think above you, and challenge your potential. At times it might be hard to break out of mediocrity especially, if you are a people's person. Success is offensive. At times making the right decision will mean hurting somebody's feelings. Your decision to advance in your life will challenge others to think about their own lives. This might lead them to their deliverance, you never know.

I remember making up my mind to do the will of God, and turn my back on my worldly friends, street gang, drug addiction, etc. It made them saw how genuine and assuredly salvation in Christ Jesus is. They all wanted what I had by all cost, as a result, many got born-again because of my decision to break out of mediocrity.

The question now is how do I get in position, alignment in order to fulfill my destiny? We will examine a character in the bible called 'Zacchaeus'.

Then Jesus entered and passed through Jericho. Now behold, there was a man named Zacchaeus who was a chief tax collector, and he was rich. And he sought to see who Jesus was, but could not because of the crowd, for he was of short stature. So he ran ahead and climbed up into a sycamore tree to see Him, for He was going to pass that way. And when Jesus came to the place, He looked up and saw him, and said to him, "Zacchaeus, make haste and come down, for today I must stay at your house." So he made haste and came down, and received Him joyfully. Luke 19:1-6 NKJV.

This man, Zacchaeus had a vision of Jesus. He must have heard a lot about him. And said within himself, one day I will see him. Only to hear that this Jesus was coming to his town, he had been nursing this desire for some time. Now is the time, this was the moment he had been waiting for. Nobody can stop him now. Do you have that kind of determination to succeed? He did everything he could to see Jesus, although he was short in stature and the crowd was the hindrance. He repositioned himself until he got what he wanted.

If you're going to be rightly positioned for your miracle, you must reposition yourself:

A. Desire: You have to be thirsty for what you need. See the picture. If you can dream it, you will do whatever it cost to receive it when the opportunity comes. Desire will prepare you for your miracle. Desire will eventually lead to determination. Determination will lead to purpose. And purpose leads to vision. Zacchaeus desired salvation, that was his drive. What is your passion?

B. Spiritually: The spirit realm rules the physical realm. You must get connected to your Creator, God, through Christ Jesus. He is the creator of all things, knows all things, and controls all things. Then submit yourself to the right spiritual leaders. You need spiritual midwives to help you with your baby. Also you need to feed on the right spiritual diet. Zacchaeus knew he needed to connect with God, he knew there is more to life than what he already had achieved.

C. Psychologically: Think differently. Stop doing what everybody is doing, do something different in order to get extraordinary result. This was exactly what Zacchaeus did. He chose not to go with the crowd. He had a different thought. As a result, he got different result.

It all start with the way you think. Your thinking will eventually affect your attitude, and eventually your way of living. The world is seeking for creative people. Whatever that makes you to busy to think is Satanic and must be destroyed in Jesus Name. Your mind is the battlefield. Fill it with God, and your life will be full of God.

CHAPTER TWO

SELF DISCOVERY

The journey to greatness begins the day you discover who you are and what you were created to do or become. No one created by God is without purpose. It's one thing to have purpose, it is another to know what that purpose is. You will never be fulfilled until you know what you are made of and made for.

God was so mindful of us when he created us. He created us to be unique with our individual personalities and destinies. This is one reason why you shouldn't compare yourself with anyone else. God created us differently. You will notice that with twin children, although, share the same birthday yet act differently. We are made differently. It's time to start celebrating that difference. The world will be so boring if we all look the same, talk alike, act the same. Diversity reveals the beauty of God in his creation.

Know Who You Are Psychologically:

Your destiny determines the way God decided to create you. Your personality was uniquely chosen to suit your assignment. Some people wonder why they act the way they do, others try to change themselves but struggle with the change. You cannot change who you are. All you need to do is to discover who you are. When you do, then you can channel your energy to the right direction. Who you are psychologically determines how you think and act.

Your personality traits affects everything about you, your career, spouse, children, studies. This is the real you behind the curtains. This is what Dr. Rick Martins called "Temperament".

Temperament is what makes us uniquely different, uniquely special. Temperament is our God-given, inborn nature; who we are on the inside. Temperament determines if we are relationship-oriented or task-oriented or goal-oriented. Temperament determines if quiet alone time gives us peace and tranquility or causes us stress and frustration. It is temperament that drives us to either be with people, or pushing us away from people.

Haven established the uniqueness of every individual. It imperative that we all know what our temperaments are. That way, we can start working our way towards fulfilling our destinies. Everyone has strengths and weaknesses. And only when you know what your strength is will you know how to build yourself up to the level you need to be. And when you know your weakness you can guard against satanic traps, and pitfalls awaiting you in this journey to greatness. All of these are tied to your temperament.

For the benefit of this study we will give an overview of each of these temperaments. More studies should be done in this area for those who wants to learn more, as we won't be able to cover all that there is regarding temperaments.

We will categorize temperaments into two groups. And each group has two sub-groups. Every individual has at least two of these.

GROUP ONE: EXTROVERT

These are the people with bubbling personalities, peoples' person and task oriented. We have two sub-groups under this category:

1. Sanguine:

People oriented, loving people, loves events, loves fun. According to Dr. Martin, "Sanguines in Inclusion are inspiring to be around. Sanguine are upbeat, optimistic, warm, friendly, and enthusiastic. When they are in the strengths of their temperament, Sanguine are never negative. Sanguines flee from negativity."

Looking at the Sanguine personality from the strength alone. You would say this is somebody I want to be with or want to flow with. Yes, they can be very attractive. But they have their weakness too.

Sanguine can be very outspoken especially when upset, their emotions runs wild and you will see the ugliness. They can swing their moods from being friendly to be disastrous. They are loud, and might not be trusted to confide in just because they are open minded people. They are dominators. Give them a little room, they dominate everyone, including conversations. If you're not the patient type, don't engage them in conversation. They will sometimes finish your sentences without thinking about it.

2. Choleric:

This group are also considered people's person, but with a difference. They are more task oriented, mostly leaders wherever they find themselves because of their ability to take responsibility, motivates others and can take risk. They are adventurous, project driven, purpose driven, goal driven, optimistic, good thinkers. Because of their nature they can be good and Pioneers, CEOs, Entrepreneurs. They are always visionary in their endeavor.

Negatively, they can be very bossy, Dr. Martin says they can "be in control of people and they will allow little or no control over their own lives or behaviors. They are not above using poor behavioral patterns to gain and maintain control over the lives and behaviors of people."

They can also be over-confidence in themselves, workaholics, users of people to achieve their goals, risk takers at the detriments of others, impatient, etc.

GROUP TWO: INTROVERT

These groups of people are the secluded. We have two sub groups:

1. Melancholy:

This group are the perfectionist. They like to get certain things done in a certain way. Dr. Martin has this to say about them, "Melancholy are thinkers. Their brains are always turned on and thinking. They analyze this. They analyze that. They over analyze almost everything. They can see pictures and images in their minds, in perfect detail and living color. Melvin and Melody Melancholy tend to be naturally negative, therefore, they tend to be moody."

The strength of a melancholy can be very attractive because of their ability to use the power of the mind. In academics they can be very research oriented. Because of their meticulous nature they can be good managers as well in their careers.

The negative side can be very dangerous as Dr. Martin cited, their critical mind can make to be somewhat judgmental, and pessimistic. They could be hard to please.

2. Phlegmatic:

This set of people are the emotionally inclined. They can be very sensitive. Dr. Martin once again has this to say regarding this group:

To the observer, the Phlegmatics are extremely slow-paced and stubborn. They allow their lives to become stagnant because it takes too much effort to use their talents.

This person goes through life doing as little as possible, quietly, and expending little energy. It is not clear whether this is because they have low energy levels, or if it is because they refuse to use what energy they do have.

Because of their sensitive nature, the Phlegmatic can be very useful spiritually, they are prone to be sensitive to the Holy Spirit because of their quietness in the inside.

All of the temperaments have its strengths and weaknesses. It will be absurd to just see somebody's strength and fall in love or see someone's weakness and be judgmental. There must be a balance. This is one major reason why people have relationship problems.

The good thing about knowing your temperament is that you can build on your strength and control your weakness. Everyone has at least two of those temperament listed above. One will be the major, and another the minor. Everyone has one from the extrovert category as well as the introvert category.

Why don't you pray to God right now to help you in the areas of your weakness, and use your strength to accomplish great things for the Kingdom of God.

Ask God to show you the reason why you are made this way, what is your assignment or calling?

DISCOVERING YOUR PURPOSE

"Before I formed you in the womb I knew you; Before you were born I sanctified you; I ordained you a prophet to the nations." Jeremiah 1:5 NKJV

Just like the above text reads. You are a pre-fix. Your life has been arranged before your conception. There is nothing more frustrating than to live life outside purpose. You are not here by chance, coincidence, or happenstance. You are here on earth because God ordained it. This has been well established in this book so far.

We will proceed further to some keys that can help you identify your purpose, calling, and assignment.

1. Destiny Prayer: In my other book, "Prayer That Touches Heaven" I expounded on the subject of prayer. There are different kinds of prayer. For those who need to know what their purpose is, You need to pray that God should unveil your destiny to you.

I love the assurance God gave regarding this kind of prayer: *"Call to Me, and I will answer you, and show you great and mighty things, which you do not know."* Jeremiah 33:3 NKJV.

There are lots of things we do not know concerning our lives. The Lord beacon on us to call, He promised to answer, and also show us those things hidden from the natural eyes, things of the future. He will reveal your purpose when you pray this kind of prayer. It is a prayer of seeking. I remember when I sought God earnestly to find what my exact purpose was on earth. My God! I was frustrated, rejected, dejected. My life was a mess. I never thought I would make it or become anything. Can you imagine the author of this book you are reading today, was a drug addict, ex-convict, gang banger, street lord, and everything in-between.

Revelation of who God is, and what my purpose is, changed everything about me. Would you do the same? Start praying, ask him to reveal himself and your purpose to you.

2. Be Yourself: Often when we come to the realization of what our purpose is, or what God has called us to do. We normally don't look like the outcome, or don't feel right. It's like presenting your resume with lots of years of experience, and a graduate degree. Yet your looks seem far from your resume. Now you can imagine what was going through Peter's head after Jesus displayed just a fraction of God's might: *"When Simon Peter saw it, he fell down at Jesus' knees, saying, "Depart from me, for I am a sinful man, O Lord!"* Luke 5:8 NKJV.

Peter knew that day, God pointed to his direction. He was always quick to say he wasn't qualified for the job, he was not the right person God is looking for. He was a unrefined when Jesus found him and qualified him. Who would have believed that the same Peter who had denied Jesus before his crucifixion will end up becoming a superstar for God. He won 3000 souls the first day he officially preached the gospel, his shadow healed the sick. Peter had a big mouth he was always quick to say something, he got into a lot of trouble. Yet God used him because he knew he wasn't qualified, therefore, yielded himself to be molded by God.

God can use anybody. You must stop trying to be who you are not. Be who you are. Let God mold you and refine you. Don't try to be an actor when you can even act. If God has called you into acting, It will be glaring because you would turn everything into a scene of act. What you do without a struggle points you towards your calling. Peter wasn't called to be fisherman. He was born into the fishing business. It was a family trade, so he thought, he could do it too. This was a big struggle for him (Luke 5).

Where have been struggling? It's time for some reality check.

3. **Celebrate Your Difference**: Until you can identify what makes you different from the next person, you are yet to find your purpose. Everyone is created differently. *"I will praise You, for I am fearfully and wonderfully made; Marvelous are Your works, And that my soul knows very well."* Psalm 139:14 from NKJV.

You can be in the same trade with somebody else, but you must be able to know what makes you, your business, different from the next person. This is what makes you unique. This is what differentiates extraordinary people from the ordinary. When you discover this, you need to start celebrating it. You have found your winning edge. Nobody can beat you to it. The devil will try to make you look awkward. That is the key. If you cannot be different, you cannot take the lead. Leaders are those who are willing to be take the risk of failing, being talked about, being misunderstood, laughed at, scorned, discouraged, yet different.

One of the ways you discover your difference is to know the problems you've been called to solve. Like Mike Murdock asserts, "Your assignment on earth is to solve a problem for somebody, somewhere and receive a reward for it. When your assignment is unrecognized, you are uncelebrated. When you are not celebrated, you are not rewarded."

What differentiates you is what you've been called to do. If you do what everybody does in the same manner, method, approach, You are yet to find your assignment. Something must be different about you. Matthew, Mark, Luke all wrote the same gospel of Jesus Christ, but they wrote from different perspectives and to different audience.

Why don't you pray and ask God to differentiate you in your assignment. Pray to be distinguished in what you do, just like Moses prayed:

Then Moses said to him, "If your presence is not going with us, don't make us leave this place. How will anyone ever know you're pleased with your people and me unless you go with us? Then we will be different from all other people on the face of the earth."

Exodus 33:15-16 GOD'S WORD TRANSLATION

CHAPTER THREE

THREE MOST IMPORTANT PEOPLE YOU NEED

The number 3 is a very significant number. It denotes divine perfection, just like the Trinity in the Godhead. God will always send you people that He wants to use to accomplish his purpose in your life or use you for them. You need 3 categories of people in your life in order to fulfill your destiny:

1. MENTOR

Again Dr. Murdock has this to say, "You can only be promoted by someone whose instructions you have followed." Who you listen to, whose advice, direction, guidance, teachings, ideas, opinion you adhere to will eventually shape your life.

Mentors are those who have gone ahead of you in the path you are treading. They are where you want to be. Mentors represent your future. They can serve as father figure to you. What makes them mentor is because you see your future in them and are willing to drink from them as they are also willing to pour into you. A Mentor will help you get to your destination faster. You will avoid mistakes on the way as a result of their godly wisdom.

"Where there is no counsel, the people fall; But in the multitude of counselors there is safety."
Proverbs 11:14. NKJV Translation

Too many people want to attain success yet they don't want to listen to others. It's like trying to write a book without reading other books. We live in a generation where people have been terribly hurt by somebody, somehow. As a result, people find it difficult to trust others. If you are in that category, I have news for you. Everyone is not the same. Your past hurt is for your future glory. Don't allow the hurt of yesterday to abort your pregnancy of greatness for tomorrow. You need people who are interested to see you succeed. Mentors, True Fathers are not easy to come by. The Holy Spirit himself places them in your life you will know when you come in contact with them. You have to run after them. Sometimes they are always busy because of their position or assignment, but it must not scare you away. You need what they carry. Chase after it like Elisha did after Elijah.

And it came to pass, when the LORD was about to take up Elijah into heaven by a whirlwind, that Elijah went with Elisha from Gilgal. Then Elijah said to Elisha, "Stay here, please, for the LORD has sent me on to Bethel." But Elisha said, "As the LORD lives, and as your soul lives, I will not leave you!" So they went down to Bethel. Now the sons of the prophets who were at Bethel came out to Elisha, and said to him, "Do you know that the LORD will take away your master from over you today?" And he said, "Yes, I know; keep silent!" Then Elijah said to him, "Elisha, stay here, please, for the LORD has sent me on to Jericho." But he said, "As the LORD lives, and as your soul lives, I will not leave you!" So they came to Jericho. Now the sons of the prophets who were at Jericho came to Elisha and said to him, "Do you know that the LORD will take away your master from over you today?" So he answered, "Yes, I know; keep silent!" Then Elijah said to him, "Stay here, please, for the LORD has sent me on to the Jordan." But he said, "As the LORD lives, and as your soul lives, I will not leave you!" So the two of them went on. And fifty men of the sons of the prophets went and stood facing them at a distance, while the two of them stood by the Jordan. Now Elijah took his mantle, rolled it up, and struck the water; and it was divided this way and that, so that the two of them crossed over on dry ground. And so it was, when they had crossed over, that Elijah said to Elisha, "Ask! What may I do for you, before I am taken away from you?" Elisha said, "Please let a double portion of your spirit be upon me." So he said, "You have asked a hard thing. Nevertheless, if you see me when I am taken from you, it shall be so for you; but if not, it shall not be so." Then it happened, as they continued on and talked, that suddenly a chariot of fire appeared with horses of fire, and separated the two of them; and Elijah went up by a whirlwind into heaven. And Elisha saw it, and he cried out, "My father, my father, the chariot of Israel and its horsemen!" So he saw him no more. And he took hold of his own clothes and tore them into two pieces. He also took up the mantle of Elijah that had fallen from him, and went back and stood by the bank of the Jordan. Then he took the mantle of Elijah that had fallen from him, and struck the water, and said, "Where is the LORD God of Elijah?" And when he also had struck the water, it was divided this way and that; and Elisha crossed over. 2 Kings 2:1-15 NKJV Translation

It doesn't matter how much grace, spiritual gifts, anointing you believe God had placed on you. You still need people who can speak into your life, stir up the gifts, help you get to your next level. Dr. Murdock says, **"There are two ways to receive wisdom: mistakes or mentors.** Mentors are the difference between poverty and prosperity; decrease and increase; loss and gain; pain and pleasure; deterioration and restoration."

God placed David under Saul for a reason. Timothy needed Apostle Paul for a reason. Who is your mentor? Some Mentors can be so far, so highly placed to reach them. That shouldn't discourage you. Read their books, listen to their teachings the anointing will flow through their materials as well as when they lay hands or prophesy on you. It's all about your faith to receive either way. God can do anything where there is faith.

Some people always think of Mentors as something more of age. That is fallacy. We've been taught that wisdom comes through age. That is somewhat true if we go by natural instinct. But spiritual wisdom has nothing to do with natural wisdom or age but grace. Jesus was 12 years old when he started displaying unusual wisdom (Luke 2:40-50).

Another fallacy taught, is that experience is the best teacher. True, experience is one of the teachers, but not the best. Revelation is the best teacher. Experience can be learned, but Revelation is given. When we go to school we learn experience and wisdom of people who had lived before us. Most times their theories are not relevant for today's generation yet we can learn from them. Revelation makes you relevant to the present generation. And only God gives that. (See Luke 5:1-11). Peter had experience but Jesus had revelation. Who became the boss?

I said all of that to say this, that choosing a mentor should not be done with the yardstick of age, but of grace, revelation, and accomplishment, you see in that person's life.

2. COLLEAGUE

This group represents your present. They are your co league. It is dangerous make a colleague a Mentor as a result of what you cherish in their lives. You will never ascend beyond mediocrity if you do that. Many do this as a result of ignorance. They may be one step ahead of you, or probably as a result of a better environment, education, connection they are better off. It still does not make them your mentor. They are to challenge you not to be complacent. These are people who should keep your enthusiasm burning with the passion for success. They will help you to hate mediocrity and challenge your gift. The difference between a Mentor and a Co-league is the level of understanding they possess concerning the things you seek or heights you desire. A younger person might have deeper understanding on a subject than an older person. It doesn't matter. It is to whom God has chosen, and endowed with revelation you need.

I remember a time in my life when God connected a fellow minister to me. Now this man had been in the ministry before me in terms of years of service. But he was still far behind in understanding some key elements to having a successful ministry. He had the anointing, but lacked knowledge. So I started coaching him in some of the things that I had learned. As soon as my dear friend started experiencing progress, I discovered the nature of relationship changed. He tried to force himself out of the friendship level to a Mentor-Father relationship. I felt used, and he lost many other relationships as a result. He became stagnant because the relationship that would have continued to supply the necessary information needed was terminated. When people try force themselves into positions God has not place them, it causes retrogression rather than progression.

When you have people like this around you need a lot of wisdom so you don't allow yourself to be offended or wounded by their actions. If not carefully handled you might end up competing with them. This will lead to distraction that eventually takes you out of purpose. The reason God puts this category of people around you is to let you know you are not alone in this race, to keep you on your toes, and help you never to be complacent. The twelve Apostles in the New Testament all had the calling of an Apostle on them, yet not all wrote books in the Bible. But they all did great things in their own rights. Colleagues are to sharpen one another, *"As iron sharpens iron, So a man sharpens the countenance of his friend."*
Proverbs 27:17 NKJV Translation.

What we see today in the Body of Christ is fellow Christians, Ministers wants to build on somebody else's weakness. We watch our fellow laborer fail and build on their failures. We are not called to compete but to complete. We are to work as the Body of Christ that is not divided. From my observation, most people who are visionless will always be competitors and often copy other people's vision, which always end in failure because that is not their calling in the first place. Remember vision keeps you focus on the mark. Spectators will always cheer who woo. You as the athlete, and must remain in your lane until you get to the finish line.

Although, we are called individually, we still have to play as a team in the Kingdom of God. All spiritual gifts, anointing, grace are needed today. No man has it all. That is why we are to be inter-dependence on one another without any room for jealousy.

You need mentors pull you up, but you need colleagues to keep you on the check, keep you on your toes.

3. PROTÉGÉ

You are not a success until you have a successor. "True success will produce a successor." God doesn't want us to just be receivers alone but to be givers as well. That has always been heaven's master plan, to reproduce. Whoever that is not reproducing is far from the blueprint of God. In a time when most people are living selfish lives it's hard to come by reproducers. We must constantly remind ourselves of God's plan: *"I will make you a great nation I will bless you And make your name great; And you shall be a blessing."* Genesis 12:2 NKJV Translation

The purpose of the blessing is to be a blessing to another. Protégé reminds you of the paths you have tread. You cannot give what you don't have. You must be blessed in order to be a blessing. One way you know your mentor as a protégé is that the story of their past fits into your present. The way you know a protégé as a mentor is that you see them today where you were yesterday. It is your duty to help them escape the deadly traps, and distractions along the way. A true Protégé takes their mentors' instructions, guidance to heart. They listen, submit, because they believe the Mentor is God's sent to them. A true Mentor takes time to invest in the life and destiny of the

Protégé because he knows he is impacting the next generation, and will be part of the next success story.

Everyone who wants to be great must be part of something greater, bigger than him. This is what drives a Protégé to a Mentor. Whoever that wants to leave a lasting legacy must be ready to invest their lives in others. This is what drives a Mentor to helping a Protégé. Every Apostle Paul needs a Timothy. And every Timothy needs an Apostle Paul.

In every stage of our callings we all go through these phases. We must be able to understand at what point, what we are or where we stand. This helps us maintain good relationship with people God brings our way. That way we don't jeopardize what God is doing in our lives on the journey to fulfillment of destiny.

It's sad sometimes how people try to force themselves to be Mentors or Fathers to people whom don't recognize their positions. People want to be served and heard. God is the one that gives promotion. On the other hand there are those who feel some are too young to handle some responsibility. Yet it is God that gives the calling not man.

Many relationships are marred as a result of lack of understanding. A colleague can try to play the role of a Mentor as a result destroy the relationship. A Protégé can feel he has arrived, therefore, he feels he doesn't need the advice, wisdom of a Mentor. There goes pride that leads to destruction. A Mentor can get jealous of a Protégé's quick success that leads to envy, which eventually leads to evil plotting. This was a typical scenario of King Saul and David. The list goes on and on.

Relationship is one of the keys to success. Knowing who you are, what role you are playing at a particular point in time in a relationship helps facilitates uncommon success. We must always remember that nobody starts at the finish line.

CHAPTER FOUR

SEPARATING THE WHEAT FROM THE CHAFF

If you're going to be great in life, you must learn and understand this principle called 'separation'. Every potential inside of you will never find expression until there is some kind of separation. This was exactly what happened in Genesis 1:

In the beginning God created the heavens and the earth. The earth was without form, and void; and darkness was on the face of the deep. And the Spirit of God was hovering over the face of the waters. Then God said, "Let there be light"; and there was light. And God saw the light, that it was good; and God divided the light from the darkness. God called the light Day, and the darkness He called Night. So the evening and the morning were the first day. Then God said, "Let there be a firmament in the midst of the waters, and let it divide the waters from the waters." Thus God made the firmament, and divided the waters which were under the firmament from the waters which were above the firmament; and it was so. And God called the firmament Heaven. So the evening and the morning were the second day. Then God said, "Let the waters under the heavens be gathered together into one place, and let the dry land appear"; and it was so. And God called the dry land Earth, and the gathering together of the waters He called Seas. And God saw that it was good. Then God said, "Let the earth bring forth grass, the herb that yields seed, and the fruit tree that yields fruit according to its kind, whose seed is in itself, on the earth"; and it was so. And the earth brought forth grass, the herb that yields seed according to its kind, and the tree that yields fruit, whose seed is in itself according to its kind. And God saw that it was good. So the evening and the morning were the third day. Then God said, "Let there be lights in the firmament of the heavens to divide the day from the night; and let them be for signs and seasons, and for days and years; and let them be for lights in the firmament of the heavens to give light on the earth"; and it was so. Then God made two great lights: the greater light to rule the day, and the lesser light to rule the night. He made the stars also. God set them in the firmament of the heavens to give light on the earth, and to rule over the day and over the night, and to divide the light from the darkness. And God saw that it was good. So the evening and the morning were the fourth day. Then God said, "Let the waters abound with an abundance of living creatures, and let birds fly above the earth across the face of the firmament of the heavens." Genesis 1:1-20 NKJV Translation

Everything God created from the beginning had potentials locked down inside of them, until God employed the principle of separation they wouldn't have fulfilled destiny or purpose of creation. We see God separating the created things in order for purpose to be accomplished. The earth was formless, without shape, purposeless. Although, buried within was greatness. It took the master to put the earth in order by way of separation.

Everything you need to achieve success in life, attain greatness is already in you from the day you were born, but it will take God to help you. Most times a lot of people are intertwined with the wrong things, wrong people, wrong career, that hinders them from advancement. Until there is a separation you will never get there. You must understand that not all are called to go with you. Not everybody can handle the next level, you might be ready for the next level, it doesn't mean all are ready. Be careful of who you carry alongside on this journey to greatness. Like Dr. Kervin Smith always say, "Success is offensive".

Learn from the life of Abraham who had a wonderful promise hanging over him, he had the prophetic word yet he struggled to see the fulfillment until there was a separation:

Then Abram went up from Egypt, he and his wife and all that he had, and Lot with him, to the South. Abram was very rich in livestock, in silver, and in gold. And he went on his journey from the South as far as Bethel, to the place where his tent had been at the beginning, between Bethel and Ai, to the place of the altar which he had made there at first. And there Abram called on the name of the LORD. Lot also, who went with Abram, had flocks and herds and tents. Now the land was not able to support them, that they might dwell together, for their possessions were so great that they could not dwell together. And there was strife between the herdsmen of Abram's livestock and the herdsmen of Lot's livestock. The Canaanites and the Perizzites then dwelt in the land. So Abram said to Lot, "Please let there be no strife between you and me, and between my herdsmen and your herdsmen; for we are brethren. Is not the whole land before you? Please separate from me. If you take the left, then I will go to the right; or, if you go to the right, then I will go to the left." And Lot lifted his eyes and saw all the plain of Jordan, that it was well watered everywhere (before the LORD destroyed Sodom and Gomorrah) like the garden of the LORD, like the land of Egypt as you go toward Zoar. Then Lot chose for himself all the plain of Jordan, and Lot journeyed east. And they separated from each other. Abram dwelt in the land of Canaan, and Lot dwelt in the cities of the plain and pitched his tent even as far as Sodom. But the men of Sodom were exceedingly wicked and sinful against the LORD.

And the LORD said to Abram, after Lot had separated from him: "Lift your eyes now and look from the place where you are—northward, southward, eastward, and westward; for all the land which you see I give to you and your descendants forever. And I will make your descendants as the dust of the earth; so that if a man could number the dust of the earth, then your descendants also could be numbered. Arise, walk in the land through its length and its width, for I give it to you."

Genesis 13:1-17 NKJV Translation

You will notice in this story that God never spoke to Abram in his journey to finding the promise land, until Lot went separate ways as way of separation. God called Abram to go not Lot. You will hinder the process to fulfillment of destiny, prophecy when you do things your own way.

It's time for some separation. You have too many bunch of chaff around you. You will never manifest your true potential until you blow the chaff out of your life. I once minister to a single lady who was believing God for a husband. I asked her about a young man I saw with her almost every time. I thought she needed God to confirm their relationship. But, she told me that there was nothing going on between them. She just seems to enjoy his company at all times. They were very good friends. I couldn't believe what I heard. I told her right there, that was the hindrance. She was shocked. I explained to her, the right man will not come to her if he kept seeing someone else around her in parties, shopping mall, grocery store. Come on. You need some space.

Listen, whatever that occupies space in your life that is not helping you to fulfill purpose, it's time to let it go. You need some space in your life. You can't be aspiring to get married yet all your friends are all single. You can't be aspiring to go to college, yet all your friends are high school graduates, drop out, or not schooled. You can't be dreaming to be a millionaire, yet you hang around people who are satisfied with minimum wage.

My God! **You can't be hanging around chicken when God has made you an 'eagle'.** Eagles don't flock. Learn the mystery of separation and you will see how quickly you will attain great heights. Who are your friends? One of the signs you see around great people, great minds is that they are not complacent. Never settle for less. Hear what Myles Munroe asserts: "Refuse to be satisfied with your last accomplishment, because potential never has a retirement plan."

Most times, when God separates the wheat from the chaff in your life, it's a painful process. It's never an easy one. It involves a lot of sacrifices, tears, determination, risk of failure, risk to be laughed at. I remember when God took me out of the street, out of gang, out of the lifestyle I thought was the only way I could live, including the wrong relationship. I thought I was going to fail. I said to myself if I don't make it I would be laughed at. That drew me closer to God in my walk with him. I remember God speaking to me in a vision these words:

"But those who wait on the LORD Shall renew their strength; They shall mount up with wings like eagles, They shall run and not be weary, They shall walk and not faint."
Isaiah 40:31 NKJV Translation

You must learn to separate yourself from everything that beclouds your life, thinking, relationship, marriage, career, family. Learn to give yourself to the Lord and your purpose will be fulfilled.

PART THREE

PURSUIT

CHAPTER ONE

UNDERSTANDING TIMES AND SEASONS

"To everything there is a season, a time for every purpose under heaven" Eccl. 3:1 NKJV

The worst thing that can happen to anyone here on earth is to go through life without knowing what time it is. Not understanding your season will cause you to abort your destiny. Some are pregnant without knowing their due date. Some don't even know that they are pregnant with purpose and wonder why the hormonal change in their lives.

Time is very crucial. Everything created is subject to time. God lives in eternity. Man and creation is subject to time. So, everything under heaven works and functions according to times and seasons. You can lose anything and get it back, but you can never lose time and get it back. That is why what you do with your time is very important.

A lot of people have asked me, why they've not been able to see the actual manifestation of the dreams they had some time back. The answer is simply 'time'. Whatever assignment, dreams, or vision you have. You need to know that it is subject to time. So what you do every second, minute, hour, day should lead towards the fulfillment of the vision. Time is great investment. You don't waste your effort on things that don't matter, because that time wasted could be spent productively. Show me what you do with your time every day and I'll tell you where you're heading. One time a lady to me for counseling, she was so frustrated because things were not going well for her family financially. Although she was a hard working woman, yet they were struggling. So I asked about her husband, and she said the husband had lost his job for some time now. And I asked, so, what is he doing now? She answered, well, he feel frustrated and seats at home playing video game. For over a year, this man has been playing video game, living his life in fantasy. That was why they were stuck.

Don't spend your time doing something unproductive. Even, if you're not getting the reward right away.

Certainly, you're investing in your future. Some people run away from schooling because they think of the years they have to spend learning. Well if you cannot invest in your career, you're not qualified to succeed. Success comes with a price. Nothing comes easy. Be ready to pay the price especially with your time.

This is where focus, determination, and discipline come in. Too many have procrastinated their destinies by pushing things that could be done today to tomorrow.

Procrastination is a deadly spiritual disease. It eats up your time until you can no longer accomplish your dream. Great accomplishers are not time wasters. They know time is investment, they don't procrastinate issues that can be resolved today to tomorrow. If you are suffering from this spiritual disease, why don't you pray for God's deliverance. Pray right now, ask God to break the yoke off your life and destiny.

"Truly I tell you, whatever you bind on earth will be bound in heaven, and whatever you loose on earth will be loosed in heaven." Matthew 18:18 NKJV Translation

Seasons of Preparation

I have often said, Miracles happens when Preparation meets opportunity. Too many people miss their divine moments because they were not prepared for it.

God takes time to prepare us for the dream he has given. The magnitude of your dream determines the weight of your preparation. Jesus spent 30 years to prepare for a 3years ministry that is still affecting the world today. It took Moses 40years to prepare for another 40years ministry. Now, it important to note that only God determines the duration of preparation for the assignment He gives.

The difference between King Saul and King David's reign was that of preparation. Saul was picked based on the pressure of the Israelites wanting a King at all cost:

Then all the elders of Israel gathered together and came to Samuel at Ramah, and said to him, "Look, you are old, and your sons do not walk in your ways. Now make us a king to judge us like all the nations." But the thing displeased Samuel when they said:

"Give us a king to judge us." So Samuel prayed to the LORD. And the LORD said to Samuel, "Heed the voice of the people in all that they say to you; for they have not rejected you, but they have rejected Me, that I should not reign over them. 1 Samuel 8:4-7 NKJV

Although, the situation of the Israelites at that time called for this because the leadership was weak. Yet, the chosen Saul didn't have the proper background on leadership, management or servant hood. He was Daddy's boy with no leadership responsibility. *"There was a man of Benjamin whose name was Kish the son of Abiel, the son of Zeror, the son of Bechorath, the son of Aphiah, a Benjamite, a mighty man of power. And he had a choice and handsome son whose name was Saul."* 1 Samuel 9:1-2 NKJV.

David's story was quite different. God used almost everything to prepare him, from his youth days to adulthood. That even the prophet Samuel would never have qualified him naturally speaking from his looks when God sent him to anoint the next King:

Now the LORD said to Samuel, "How long will you mourn for Saul, seeing I have rejected him from reigning over Israel? Fill your horn with oil, and go; I am sending you to Jesse the Bethlehemite. For I have provided Myself a king among his sons."And Samuel said, "How can I go? If Saul hears it, he will kill me." But the LORD said, "Take a heifer with you, and say, 'I have come to sacrifice to the LORD.' Then invite Jesse to the sacrifice, and I will show you what you shall do; you shall anoint for Me the one I name to you." So Samuel did what the LORD said, and went to Bethlehem. And the elders of the town trembled at his coming, and said, "Do you come peaceably?" And he said, "Peaceably; I have come to sacrifice to the LORD. Sanctify yourselves, and come with me to the sacrifice." Then he consecrated Jesse and his sons, and invited them to the sacrifice. So it was, when they came, that he looked at Eliab and said, "Surely the LORD's anointed is before Him!" But the LORD said to Samuel, "Do not look at his appearance or at his physical stature, because I have refused him. For the LORD does not see as man sees; for man looks at the outward appearance, but the LORD looks at the heart." So Jesse called Abinadab, and made him pass before Samuel. And he said, "Neither has the LORD chosen this one." Then Jesse made Shammah pass by. And he said, "Neither has the LORD chosen this one." Thus Jesse made seven of his sons pass before Samuel. And Samuel said to Jesse, "The LORD has not chosen these." And Samuel said to Jesse, "Are all the young men here?" Then he said, "There remains yet the youngest, and there he is, keeping the sheep." And Samuel said to Jesse, "Send and bring him. For we will not sit down till he comes here." So he sent and brought him in. Now he was ruddy, with bright eyes, and good-looking. And the LORD said, "Arise, anoint him; for this is the one!" 1 Samuel 16:1-12

It takes a man who can lead the sheep, protect the sheep, fight for the sheep in the wilderness to also lead God's people as King at that time. Such was David's resume for kingship. That was why his reign was totally different from that of Saul.

God takes time to give us the necessary background, foundation we need for the future project. Most times when we are in our season of preparation, it often feels as if nothing is happening, it feels boring, slow, frustration. Nobody likes to wait. But it pays at the end. Like Andrew Stanley asserts: "Waiting time is not wasted time for anyone in whose heart God has placed a vision. Difficult time. Painful. Frustrating time. But not wasted time."

Waiting time is not an idle time. You need to be busy in your time of waiting for fulfillment. That is your season of preparation. Get involved in something reasonable, valuable, invest wisely, serve faithfully. Learn with passion. Where ever, whatever you find yourself doing at that time. Do it with all your heart. You must be pro-active.

Preparation is never a once in a life occurrence. Every level in your assignment calls for another season of preparation. Any time God isolates you within your busy-ness. He wants you to put yourself together for the next level. You must not mess with that time out. You might not get it back. When the promotion comes you will be helpless not knowing how to handle it. Never see yourself as one that has arrived, keep learning, keep growing, keep listening.

CHAPTER TWO

FAILURE OR CATALYST

I have come to the realization that the reason why many would not take risk to get to the next level is because they are afraid of failure. Nobody wants to fail. Everyone wants to succeed, but failure is part of success. Every great man or woman had experienced failure at one point in their lives. See what Henry Blackaby asserts:

> Failure is a powerful force in the making of a leader. The failure itself is not the issue; it's what failure leads to that is so determinative in leadership development. For true leaders, failure will not destroy them but will, instead, further develop their character.

So many of history's great leaders suffered major failures, crises, and disappointments in their development as leaders that these traumas almost seem prerequisite to leadership success. If any conclusion can be drawn from the biographies of great leaders, it is that none enjoyed easy paths to greatness. It could, in fact, be argued that, had they avoided hardship, greatness would also have eluded them. This painful process of leadership development may be seen in the lives of biblical leaders as well. Moses, arguably the greatest figure in the Old Testament, had a life filled with adversity and failure. As a newborn, his life was threatened, so his mother gave him away to a foreigner. Although Moses was raised among Egyptian royalty, he was regularly reminded that his ancestry was, in fact, slavery. His bungled attempt to rescue a fellow Hebrew meant he had to flee for his life into the desert. Moses spent forty years herding sheep in the wilderness for his father-in-law because of a mistake he made in his youth. He spent another forty years wandering in the wilderness because of a mistake made by those he was leading. He would ultimately die outside the land he had dreamed of entering because of a mistake he made while wandering in the wilderness. Yet, despite his significant failures, even secular historians recognize Moses as one of the most influential leaders of all time.

If you will be great in life, you must be ready to take risk. Failure is not the end of one's life. It only teaches you what does not work. So, try again using another method, approach, style, etc. People who die a failure are those who refuse to learn from their mistakes. Remember, we are not perfect people. We imperfect people serving a perfect God striving to become perfect like our God through the help and power of his Spirit. Our total dependence is on Him.

"I can do all things through Christ who strengthens me." Philippians 4:13 NKJV.

Based on the above premise, we can deduce that when we fail in our duties, it simply means we did it in our flesh, using our minds only. God cannot fail, we need to learn how to allow God to help us in all our endeavors, whether secular or spiritual, in your marriage, relationship, raising your children, career decision, workplace, project, etc.

Dr. Kervin Smith asserts that we must look beyond ourselves. In his words, "Unfortunately, this is the direction our culture has convinced many people to take, dissuading them from trusting in God and encouraging them to rely only on themselves and their own efforts."

A typical example of one who relied on himself was Peter:

Now in the fourth watch of the night Jesus went to them, walking on the sea. And when the disciples saw Him walking on the sea, they were troubled, saying, "It is a ghost!" And they cried out for fear. But immediately Jesus spoke to them, saying, "Be of good cheer! It is I; do not be afraid." And Peter answered Him and said, "Lord, if it is You, command me to come to You on the water." So He said, "Come." And when Peter had come down out of the boat, he walked on the water to go to Jesus. But when he saw that the wind was boisterous, he was afraid; and beginning to sink he cried out, saying, "Lord, save me!" And immediately Jesus stretched out His hand and caught him, and said to him, "O you of little faith, why did you doubt?" And when they got into the boat, the wind ceased. Matthew 14:22-32 NKJV

It was Jesus who invited Peter in the first instance, and Peter did the miraculous as a result. Now, that is what faith can deliver to you, the supernatural. Faith releases the power for exploit. But, along the way, Peter took his eyes off the one who made it possible, got carried away. All of a sudden he started sinking. Many are sinking today, because their eyes is off the make, provider, the sustainer, God himself. Peter was smart enough to realize that Jesus did not invite him to fail but to succeed. He cried out for help, and was rescued. Where are you in your walk with him?

Wherever you are right now, would you ask him to help you and ignore pride or what your mind is saying to you?

God is not interested in our failures. He is much interested in our success. That is where He takes his glory. He is interested in everything about our lives, He cares for his children. We must learn to trust him.

Another fallacy I have heard from people who don't want to take risk is because of what others would say. What would people say? This is a common saying and mindset of a mediocre. The truth of the matter is people will always talk either ways, good or bad. So, why must you live your life by what people say. We are to live by what God says and that alone. Most times what God says is always contrary to what the circumstances presents to our very natural eyes. This is where fear comes in. What God says is what brings faith, *"So then faith comes by hearing, and hearing by the word of God."* Romans 10:17 NKJV.

Faith is not the absence of fear. Fear reveals the weakness of your flesh, and draws you closer to God who is able to help. Faith drives you to take the risk, in taking risk based on the spoken word of God is what eventually brings success.

Success comes with a price. It's never a smooth ride. It involves you at times doing the wrong thing before doing what is right. You must not be stuck in yesterday's failures. "Those who hang on to their past are doomed to unnecessary cycles of failure and mediocrity."

Getting back up again could be difficult after going through failure, hurts, disappointments. Our society is filled with people who have a past, that some don't like to talk about. Abusive relationship, broken marriage, abuse of children, ex-convict, ex-drug addict, ex-alcoholic, etc. Everyone, one way or the other is an ex-something. I must not be judged by my past. The fact that I am what I am today, and not stuck in my yesterday, signifies that I am victorious over my past. That is success.

If you get stuck in yesterday's issues, You will never attain success. Because you will limit yourself, limit God, and end up denying your destiny. The enemy (Satan) doesn't want you to get up again. He wants you to feel you can never make it again. I got good news for you, although, you've messed up in the past. But your future is always brighter, greater, better than your past. Now is the time to bounce back up.

My life is a typical example. God delivered me from the street gang, alcohol, drugs. I felt I was a failure, that I would never amount to anything. Almost, everyone around me gave up on me. Even became a fugitive at one time. Do you know, because of my experiences and convictions of who God is and is able to do with an 'ex' like what he did with Apostle Paul in the New Testament. I stood my ground and declared over my life, I will make it, my story must change. Today, God is using me, and my story to influence many lives all around the world, that is why you are reading this book.

It's amazing what God can do with your past failures if you give it to him. Your past eventually becomes the catalyst for your success. I rarely listen to people who have nothing to say about their past. You can't be relevant to this present generation if you have not been there, done that.

I challenge you in the name of Jesus Christ to get back up, turn around, take your eyes of the past failures and look towards your future and see great and mighty things awaiting you as you take the step of faith. *"For I know the thoughts that I think toward you, says the LORD, thoughts of peace and not of evil, to give you a future and a hope."* Jeremiah 29:11 NKJV.

CHAPTER THREE

EVALUATING THE VISION

What keeps a vision alive is not having continuous momentum, or vigorous enthusiasm. But the ability to evaluate one's self, and the vision. Vision is likened to a vehicle which is designed for movement. One can drive for as long as the gas can take you. If you refuse to refill, it will eventually stop moving, if you refuse to do the oil change or other mechanical checks, your engine will be running at risk and eventually crash someday.

Too many people started well but along the line, they lost it. To start a vision is not the issue, but maintaining the vision is critical. At every time, you must come to a time where you need to pause, think, strategize. Our culture is an ever changing one. You can afford to run your business like it was 10 years ago. You must know what works today, and what doesn't work. You must be ready to get rid of old baggage, and engage the new world. All of these comes as a result of evaluation.

Not evaluating the vision have made a lot of business go out of business. Statistics prove that most new businesses die within the first 3 years. That can be avoided, if we will take time out. Go back to the drawing table. At times, evaluation helps you to take a different approach, never be too rigid to try something new. The language of today's generation in organizational leadership is packaging & strategic planning. You can have the right message, right product, yet not reaching your audience if you're not well packaged, and not strategic in your approach.

Evaluation will take you there. The key to continuous success is continuous improvement. Never get to the point of complacency. There is always room for improvement.

Few years ago, a major auto company known as General Motors went into bankruptcy. Many thought that was their end. But it was a time out for them, it was time to re-evaluate, and strategize on how to get back up and beyond where they used to be. Today they are back on the chart in productivity, improvement, and sales. Read this excerpt taken from an auto sales article:

General Motors' annual conference with investors and financial analysts Tuesday sent the message that the automaker, which emerged from Chapter 11 bankruptcy just over two years ago, has demonstrated improvement but has a long-term plan for substantially more progress to be made. The plan, GM Chairman and CEO Dan Akerson told the audience, has "all the requisites to push this company from good to great." The pillars of the plan are: design, build and sell the world's best vehicles; strengthen brand value; grow profitably globally (profits over market share); and maintain a "fortress" balance sheet that weathers the ups and downs of the economy and auto sales.

Every Visionary, Pioneer, CEO, Entrepreneur, must take time out for re-evaluation and improvement to remain standing in this challenging & competitive age.

CONCLUSION

HOLDING ON TO THE SOURCE

I am the vine, you are the branches. He who abides in Me, and I in him, bears much fruit; for without Me you can do nothing. If anyone does not abide in Me, he is cast out as a branch and is withered; and they gather them and throw them into the fire, and they are burned. If you abide in Me, and My words abide in you, you will ask what you desire, and it shall be done for you. By this My Father is glorified, that you bear much fruit; so you will be My disciples. John 15:5-8 NKJV.

God does not only want us to succeed. He desires that we remain successful. All the strategy and human development programs are good ideas. But will not last outside God. When we bring our natural ideas to the table before God and acknowledge that He is the source of all knowledge. He causes us to be more productive. The river that ignores its source will eventually dry up. The more we abide in him, the more we drink of him. If He has the ability to sustain creation till date, He also has the ability to sustain any vision He has given you. The vision will not survive outside the one who gave the vision.

"Unless the LORD builds the house, They labor in vain who build it, Unless the LORD guards the city, The watchman stays awake in vain."
Psalm 127:1 NKJV.

It is very easy to get carried away with trying to build the vision by ourselves, forgetting that it has a source. God will always furnish us with divine ideas that can whether natural storms, disasters. He knows what tomorrow holds. A wise person with a dream will hold on to the one who can sustain that dream.

As I conclude this writing. I am holding on to Him who is able to help me fulfill all He has placed within me. God is my source of strength and in Him I live, in Him, I trust, in Him, will I succeed.

Would you make that you confession today.

Father I pray for all my readers, all you have placed great dreams, visions, ideas in them. I ask Lord that you will cause them to succeed. Grant them victory over dream killers, vision stealers. Father uphold them as they go through their process of incubation, formation, and manifestation in Jesus Mighty Name.

Lord let these words they have read and heard sink deeply beyond their minds to their spirits, and let it bear fruits, and much more fruits for your name sake.

Be glorified in the lives of my readers in Jesus Name. Amen.

BIBLOGRAPHY

1. Munroe, Myles. Becoming A Leader. New Kensington, Whitaker House. 2009

2. Graham, John. Importance of Vision. www.johngrahamspeaker.org. 2010

3. Martin, Rick. God Created You, Dundee, Cook Communication. 2004

4. Ibid, Pg.15

5. Ibid, Pg. 152

6. Ibid, Pg. 65

7. Ibid, Pg. 122

8. Murdock, Mike. The Law of Recognition. Forth Worth, The Wisdom Center. 2007

9. Ibid

10. Ibid

11. Ibid

12. Munroe, Myles. Understanding Your Potential. Shippensburg, Destiny Image Publishers, Inc. 2002

13. Stanley, Andy. Visioneering. New York, Multnomah Books. 1999

14. Blackaby, Henry T. (2001). Spiritual Leadership: Moving People on to God's Agenda. Broadman & Holman Publishers. Kindle Edition.

15. Ibid pg.41

16. Smith, Kervin J. Your Destiny Now. Eden Praire, Kervin J. Smith Ministries. 2009

17. Ibid. Pg. 24

18. Edmunds Auto Observer. "GM Grades Itself As "Shows Improvement" By Michelle Krebs August 10, 2011

Other Books By Dr. George Agbonson

Journey of Faith

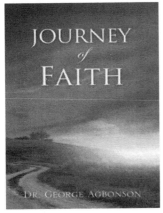

Prayer that touches Heaven

Contact:

Christ Restoration Ministries Int'L.
U.S.A
www.christrestoration.net
Email: admin@christrestoration.net